THE SHAMBHALA GUIDE TO AIKIDŌ

Morihei Ueshiba (1883–1969), the founder of Aikidō

THE
SHAMBHALA GUIDE TO
AIKIDŌ

John Stevens

SHAMBHALA
Boston & London
1996

Shambhala Publications, Inc.
Horticultural Hall
300 Massachusetts Avenue
Boston, Massachusetts 02115

9 8 7 6 5 4 3 2 1

First Edition
Printed in the United States of America
⊗ This edition is printed on acid-free paper that meets
the American National Standards Institute Z39.48 Standard.
Distributed in the United States by Random House, Inc.,
and in Canada by Random House of Canada Ltd

Library of Congress Cataloging-in-Publication Data
Stevens, John, 1947–
    The Shambhala guide to Aikidō / John Stevens.—1st ed.
        p.   cm.
    Includes bibliographical references and index.
    ISBN 1-57062-170-5 (alk. paper)
    1. Aikido.   2. Aikido—Training.   I. Title.
GV1114.35.S776   1996   95-49996
796.8'154—dc20   CIP

Contents

Preface

AIKIDŌ, the "Way of Harmony," is an art of integration, a new and revolutionary discipline founded by Morihei Ueshiba (1883–1969), perhaps history's greatest warrior, who discovered that applied nonviolence is one of the most potent weapons human beings possess.

Aikidō is not easy to define—it is more than a martial art, it is not a competitive sport, and it is a spiritual discipline but not a religion. *The Shambhala Guide to Aikidō* is an introduction to the rich culture of Aikidō, and the book outlines and illustrates the Aikidō experience. It begins with a short biography of the founder of Aikidō, Morihei Ueshiba, whose photograph graces every Aikidō training hall. The exciting story of Morihei's quest for the true meaning of the Way of a Warrior is a continual inspiration for students of Aikidō. Also, to properly understand the techniques and philosophy of Aikidō, it is essential to be familiar with the genesis of the art and the milieu in which it emerged.

Chapter 2 describes the traditional training methods and techniques of the art of Aikidō. Chapter 3 is a presentation of the profound philosophy and ideals of Aikidō, as conceived by Master Ueshiba, and includes a selection of some of his principal teachings at the end of the chapter. The book concludes with several shorter chapters of reference: Styles and Schools of Aikidō, Resources, and a Glossary.

The Shambhala Guide to Aikidō is based on experiences that I have shared with Aikidō practitioners all over the world. It is my sincere hope that *The Shambhala Guide to Aikidō* will be the first book that Aikidō instructors recommend to beginning students, as well as the one that Aikidō practitioners present to their parents, friends, co-workers, partners, and spouses when confronted with the question, "What is Aikidō?"

Acknowledgments

Heartfelt thanks to: Kisshōmaru Ueshiba for permission to reproduce photographs from the Ueshiba family collection; Gaetan Francken for taking most of the technical photographs; Jan Watson, Susan Perry, Remi Baptiste, Allen Beebe, Paul McLaughlin, Alan Nagahisa, and Michael Reichman for additional photographs; Susan Perry and Ron Rubin for advice and assistance with the "Resources" section; and to my students and friends who appear in the illustrations: Domien Moons, Wilbert Sluiter, Isaac Reawaruw, Michael Reichman, Staf Costermans, Jo Schops, Jos VanHaegenborgh, Ton Albertz, Mirjam Paalvast, An Vermeire, Rufin Bouwens, Dominique Veekmans, Richard Bremer, Brigitte Souilljee, Douwe Hendriksma, Yosuke Yoshida, Hugh Gribben, Roger Kwok, Jorge Delva, Ron Rubin, and Mark Adachi.

Thanks too to Samuel Bercholz, Kendra Crossen, Brian Boland, Peter Turner, and the rest of the Shambhala family for their constant encouragement and support.

The Shambhala Guide to Aikidō

1
Morihei Ueshiba, the Founder of Aikidō

THE PHENOMENON known as Aikidō originated with Morihei Ue-shiba, an extraordinarily skilled and profoundly spiritual master born in Japan in 1883. Morihei, commonly referred to as Ō-Sensei (Great Teacher) by Aikidō students, grew up in Tanabe City. Tanabe, located in Wakayama Prefecture, is about two hundred miles south of Ōsaka, situated along the Pacific Ocean and bordering the mountain mandala of Kumano. Kumano is believed to be the sacred space where the Shintō gods first touched the earth; it is also the site of Mount Kōya, the citadel of Shingon Buddhism founded by the wonder-worker Kūkai in the ninth century. The mountains, forests, streams, waterfalls, caverns, craggy rocks, and shrines of Kumano seem to partake of a particular divinity, and Kumano is often described as not simply a place but a state of mind where "god and nature are one."

In addition to their piety, the people of Tanabe are characterized as hard working, stubborn, and possessed of explosive tempers, traits that Morihei displayed throughout his life. Although there were no samurai left in the region by the time of Morihei's birth, the Ueshiba clan had been warriors in the past, and many of Morihei's ancestors were renowned for their great physical strength. Morihei, though,

1

was a bit small at birth and rather sickly as a child. The only boy in the household, Morihei was doted on by his parents and four sisters.

As he grew older, Morihei became more active and built up his body. Working on the local fishing boats, he learned to wield a harpoon, and he took up sumō wrestling. Morihei did a lot of hiking in the Kumano mountains as well, on occasion with the extra burden of an infirm pilgrim loaded on his back. Morihei was quick-witted and loved to read, but he did not like being cooped up in a classroom, so he left middle school in his first year. Even though he abandoned formal schooling, Morihei continued his studies of esoteric Buddhism at a local Shingon temple, memorizing the various rites and chants. Much of Morihei's early education consisted of learning from nature as he swam and fished in the ocean and trekked in the mountains; he later declared, "No matter where I am, part of me always remains absorbed in the sacred space of Kumano."

After mastering the *soroban* (abacus), Morihei secured a job as an accountant at the prefectural tax office. This work did not suit him (Morihei often sided with the taxpayers against the government), so, in 1901, Yoroku sent his eighteen-year-old son off to the great metropolis of Tōkyō, in hope that Morihei would establish himself in a suitable career. Morihei actually did quite well as a merchant in the capital, and he formally began the practice of several martial arts, but his heart was not in commerce, and soon he was back in Tanabe. In 1902, he married Hatsu Itogawa, a distant relative, and prepared to enlist in the army.

As soon as Japan began to modernize, the new Meiji government got entangled in the various "great games" being played out in that part of the globe. The major European countries, the United States, China, and then upstart Japan were all vying for power in Asia. The Japanese fought a war with China in 1894–1895 and surprised everyone, including themselves, by winning. When Morihei returned to Tanabe, Japan was gearing up for war with Russia. Morihei flunked the initial physical exam because of his height: he was less than the required five feet, two inches tall. Mortified by this rejection, Morihei took to hanging from trees with heavy weights attached to his legs to stretch himself the necessary one-half inch.

Successful on his next physical, Morihei was assigned to a Wakayama infantry regiment. The competitive Morihei relished the discipline of military life. Simply finishing at the head of a forced march was not good enough for Morihei—he had to accomplish that feat handicapped by the extra packs he had picked up from stragglers. During his military service, Morihei practiced more martial arts, becoming extremely proficient at sumō wrestling, bayonet and sword fighting.

After war with Russia broke out in 1904, Morihei was not sent to the front with the rest of his regiment. His father, Yoroku, who was a politician with certain connections, secretly requested that his only son be kept from the fighting. Morihei, however, insisted that he be sent overseas, and the young soldier was dispatched to the Manchurian front in 1905. It is not clear how much action Morihei saw in China; at any rate, he returned to Tanabe unscathed at the end of the war. Impressed by his enthusiasm, several of Morihei's superiors asked him to consider a career in the military. Morihei declined, for even at that young age, as he later recalled, "I instinctively felt that there was something terribly wrong about combat; there are no real winners in a war, there is only death and destruction."

After his discharge from the military, Morihei's life had no direction. He began to act strangely, shutting himself in his room for hours, disappearing in the woods for days, or standing on the beach baring himself to the full brunt of a typhoon. He dabbled in various martial arts during this period, and whenever there was rice-cake pounding (a communal event in Japanese villages), Morihei swung the heavy pestle with such manic fury that he shattered it. He did this so often that he was not allowed to participate anymore. To build up his strength, Morihei stacked his shoulder pole with four or five times the normal load, but by doing so he blocked the narrow roads of the village, creating another nuisance for his neighbors.

In 1909 the troubled Morihei came under the beneficial influence of Kumagusu Minakata (1867–1941). Like Morihei, Minakata had dropped out of school early, but he was among the first group of Japanese permitted to travel overseas. He attended college briefly in the United States, and then he again dropped out and took off to travel around the Americas and the West Indies. In 1892, Minakata settled in England, where he worked at the British Museum, mostly doing research in natural sciences. A self-taught polymath, Minakata learned English, French, Latin, Arabic, and Chinese, and over the years he published nearly three hundred articles in international scientific journals.

After eighteen years abroad, Minakata returned to Tanabe. The eccentric scholar Minakata teamed up with the energetic Morihei to spearhead what was likely modern Japan's first environmental protest movement. In 1906, the Meiji government promulgated the Edict on Shrine Amalgamation, a scheme that called for the consolidation of smaller local shrines with bigger national ones. Once that was accomplished, the government planned to appropriate the property of the local shrines, sell off the timber for a big profit, and "develop" the land. Minakata argued, correctly, that once the local shrines were razed and the woods cut down, there would be no place for birds to nest; pesky insects would increase, and farmers would have to resort to the use of costly and dangerous insecticides. Furthermore, watersheds would be destroyed, the bay would become polluted, and fishermen would lose their livelihoods.

In the end, Minakata and Morihei's protest movement proved effective, and Tanabe lost very few shrines. Morihei later remarked: "Minakata was a great man, and he taught me the importance of standing up for the rights of ordinary people and their land." And although he did not refer to himself as such, Morihei remained a keen environmentalist throughout his life.

Despite the success of the protest movement, the economy of Wakayama became more and more depressed—there was not enough land or work to support the second and third sons of local families. Morihei was eager to set out on a new course, so in 1912, staked by his father and another wealthy relative, Morihei headed up a group of eighty-four settlers who journeyed to Shirataki, deep in the heart of distant Hokkaidō.

The settlers had to start from scratch in the Hokkaidō wilderness, and Morihei was tireless in his promotion of the colony. He cleared the land, he lumbered, he constructed buildings, he grew crops, he raised hogs, he organized health and sanitation brigades, he served on the community council. Morihei continued to practice martial arts in Hokkaidō, often engaging in impromptu sumō contests and other tests of strength. Morihei remained undefeated until he crossed paths with the legendary Sōkaku Takeda (1859–1943).

Sōkaku, described by Morihei as "the last of the oldtime warriors," loved battlefields. Born in Aizu, home of the fiercest warriors in Japan, Sōkaku was taught to fight with his hands, a sword, and a spear by his severe samurai father from a very early age. As a child, Sōkaku entertained himself by hiding in the bushes and watching the carnage that ensued as the die-hard Aizu clan loyalists battled the Imperial forces. After the Aizu clan was defeated, the young Sōkaku took off and waged his own private war against the top martial artists and street fighters of Japan. He roamed as far south as Okinawa and as far north as Hokkaidō, challenging every martial artist he encountered to a duel and taking on all comers in the streets, not infrequently with fatal results for his adversaries.

Sōkaku paid a dear price for acquiring such fearsome prowess. Pursued by the friends and disciples of those he had killed in combat, Sōkaku's life was in constant danger. When Sōkaku saw another human being, he saw the threat of imminent death. After Sōkaku's sword was taken away from him by the authorities (he had cut down a number of construction workers in a melee), Sōkaku armed himself with a walking stick containing a hidden blade, and he concealed an unsheathed knife in his kimono. Every time he left home, he warned

Morihei around the age of thirty-two when he first began training with Sōkaku Takeda in Hokkaidō.

his family, "Don't expect me back." Sōkaku would not enter a building, even his own house, without first calling out and waiting until someone he recognized appeared to escort him in, and he would not take any food or drink until someone else had tested it first to ensure that it had not been poisoned. Sōkaku slept with a knife and iron fan, and he shifted his bedding several times a night to confuse would-be attackers. When he did sleep, he often cried out in terror, haunted by the faces of the people he had slain.

Given his reputation as a peerless martial artist, Sōkaku was in great demand as an instructor to the military and to the police. The Hokkaidō frontier was overrun with outlaws, and Sōkaku had been summoned there to help police establish law and order in the volatile province. At the time, Sōkaku was teaching what he called Daitō-Ryū Aiki Jūjutsu. In March 1915, after being handled with ease by Sōkaku, Morihei enrolled in a ten-day Daitō-Ryū training course that Sōkaku was teaching at an inn in Engaru, and then he immediately signed up for another ten-day session. Morihei spent the next four years under Sōkaku's unremittingly severe tutelage.

Morihei once said, "I practiced over thirty martial arts—most for less than three months!" That is, he was able to master most techniques very quickly. Daitō-Ryū Aiki Jūjutsu was the discipline Morihei studied the longest, and that art had the greatest influence on the technical development of Aikidō.

However, Morihei's quest was always primarily spiritual rather than martial, and although he gained much from Sōkaku, he was still searching for something deeper than expert technique and devastating power. In December 1919, when a telegram arrived informing Morihei of his father's grave illness back in Tanabe, he turned over his property to Sōkaku and left Hokkaidō for good.

Instead of heading directly back to Tanabe, Morihei, for some reason, detoured to Ayabe, headquarters of the Ōmoto-kyō sect. There he encountered the grand shaman Onisaburō Deguchi (1871–1947), and Morihei's life took another dramatic turn. Morihei was enthralled by the cosmic theology espoused by Onisaburō, who emphasized the innate divinity of each and every human being; Onisaburō, in turn, immediately recognized Morihei's sincerity and tremendous potential.

Morihei lingered on in Ayabe for several days, and by the time he arrived back in Tanabe, his father had died (as Onisaburō had prophesied). Despite the fierce opposition of his mother and his wife (Morihei and his wife had two small children, a girl and a boy, and she was expecting a third), Morihei moved to Ayabe and joined Ōmoto-kyō.

At Ayabe, Morihei practiced Ōmoto-kyō meditation techniques,

Morihei, around age thirty-eight, sitting in his first dōjō, built for him on the Ōmoto-kyō compound in Ayabe, near Kyōto. Thickset and ferocious looking after several years of hard-edged Daitō Ryū Aiki Jūjutsu training under Sōkaku, Morihei subsequently had spiritual revelations that would gradually transform his art into Aikidō, the Way of Harmony.

learned *kototama* chanting, and studied poetry and calligraphy—a cardinal tenet of Ōmoto-kyō is that "art equals religion." Morihei was put in charge of the compound's extensive organic gardens— care of the environment and the growing of healthy, pesticide-free food was another essential tenet of Ōmoto-kyō. A small dōjo (train- ing hall) was built for him to teach martial arts to Ōmoto-kyō follow- ers, a group that included many senior military officers, mostly navy men. The first year in Ayabe was a great trial for Morihei; his second son was born in April 1920, but he lost both boys to illness later that year. Fortunately, in 1921 his wife gave birth to a healthy baby boy, Kisshōmaru, who was Morihei's sole surviving son.

Sōkaku turned up in Ayabe in the spring of 1922. Whether Sōkaku was invited by Morihei or showed up on his own accord is a matter

Morihei with Onisaburō Deguchi and a group of Ōmoto-kyō followers. Onisaburō's eclectic esotericism—a heady mix of ancient Shintō, Taoism, Tantric Buddhism, and Western gnosticism—and his teaching that "art equals religion" had a profound influence on the creation of Morihei's Aikidō.

of contention. Onisaburō did not hide his disapproval of Sokaku: "This man reeks of blood and violence," he said. The Ōmoto-kyō people were greatly relieved when Sōkaku finally left the Ayabe compound six months later. Although Sōkaku and Morihei met several times over the ensuing years, Morihei gradually distanced himself from Sokaku, and he began to modify substantially the techniques he had learned from the Daitō Ryū grandmaster.

Perhaps the turning point of Morihei's career as a martial artist was his quixotic trip in 1924 to Mongolia with Onisaburō in search of Shambhala, the fabled kingdom of heaven on earth. For much of the five-month adventure, Morihei was face to face with death, battling bandits, renegade soldiers, and the Chinese army. Onisaburō, Morihei, and the rest of their party were eventually placed in detention by the Chinese military and narrowly escaped summary execution. Released into the custody of the Japanese consul, the party returned safely to Japan in July of 1924.

Once back in Ayabe, Morihei resumed his training with an intensity that both amazed and alarmed his friends and students. Energy seemed to swirl about him; doors and windows would rattle when he entered a room. He trained outdoors in the woods almost every night, and he also disappeared for a time in the mountains of Kumano. One spring day in 1925, the forty-two-year-old Morihei was challenged to a fight by a navy officer visiting Ayabe. The officer, armed with a wooden sword, was unable to touch Morihei. After the officer conceded defeat, Morihei went into his garden to douse his face with cold water from the well. Suddenly, Morihei felt enveloped by golden light: "I saw the divine," he later recalled. "All at once I understood the nature of creation: the way of a warrior is to manifest divine love, a spirit that embraces and nurtures all things."

After this transforming experience, Morihei manifested superhuman, even miraculous, powers. In addition to such uncanny feats as felling ten men with a single shout and scoring a hole in one the first and only time he swung a golf club, Morihei demonstrated the incredible ability to dodge bullets—he faced off against a military firing squad (twice!), and they were not able to hit him. As well as enabling him to anticipate any kind of attack, Morihei's clairvoyance had practical application as well. Once, for example, in the middle of a training session, he suddenly told one of disciples, "There is a gentleman dressed in a black kimono wandering around trying to find this place. Go and fetch him here." The disciple went outside and soon discovered a gentleman in a black kimono. "Excuse me," the man said. "I'm trying to locate the Ueshiba Dōjō . . ."

Morihei, around age forty-seven, when the Kōbukan opened in Wakamatsu-chō section of Tōkyō. The Kōbukan was nicknamed "The Hell Dōjō" for the severity and thoroughness of the practice sessions conducted there. However, one of the principal students of that era, Yoshimi Yonekawa, once remarked, "It wasn't hell, it was heaven, because Ueshiba Sensei was always with us and the training was so wonderful."

Not surprisingly, word quickly spread of the "martial art wizard," and all manner of fighters came to test Morihei for themselves. Morihei sent every single challenger flying, and by the time he opened his Kōbukan Dōjō in 1931 in Tōkyō, he had acquired a large following of fervent supporters, consisting mainly of the nation's military and political elite. His personal students (including several women), selected after careful screening, were the cream of the crop. During this period Morihei's art was usually referred to as Aiki-Budō.

Although Morihei had largely separated himself from the Ōmoto-kyō organization (with Onisaburō's blessing: "Your mission is to teach the real way of the warrior to the world," Onisaburō told Morihei), in 1935 he was implicated in the second Ōmoto-kyō incident. (Onisaburō had been arrested once before in 1921.) The increasingly repressive authorities were suspicious of Onisaburō's anticapitalist, pacifist, and antiimperialist stance (Ōmoto-kyō envisioned an egalitarian society free of emperors and government), and they arrested him and the rest of the Ōmoto-kyō leadership on the charge of lèse-majesté. The Ōmoto-kyō compound in Ayabe was razed and the organization banned. A warrant was issued for Morihei as well, but he was shielded from arrest by several of his disciples in the police agency. Nevertheless, Morihei was interrogated, and it appears he was under house arrest for a brief period.

After lying low for a while, Morihei resumed his position as senior instructor to the main military academies in Tōkyō and Ōsaka. Morihei was, in fact, one of the most important and influential people in

Morihei demonstrating Aiki-Budō: (*top*) this is one of the photos taken at the Noma Dōjō in 1936 when Morihei was fifty-two. Such *hanmi-handachi* ("half-seated, half-standing") techniques are still practiced today in Aikidō dōjō. In the prewar years, training was geared more to actual combat (*bottom*); this photo, taken from Morihei's manual *Budō*, published in 1938, shows a countermove against a bayonet attack.

Japan at that time. He was, in effect, the government's minister of Budō (martial arts). A hand-drawn instruction manual called *Budō Renshū* was privately circulated in 1933, an extraordinary film documentary (in which Morihei throws wave after wave of attackers) shot in Ōsaka in 1935, and another technical manual, *Budō*, containing professional photographs of Morihei demonstrating Aiki-Budō techniques, was published in 1938. In addition, Morihei also posed for three thousand technical photographs taken at the Noma Dōjō (operated by Seiji Noma, president of Japan's largest publishing house, Kōdansha) in 1936.

Fighting with China broke out in 1937, and Japan began its headlong descent into the hell of World War II. Morihei remained in active government service during the initial years of the war, but he became deeply disturbed by the increasing brutality and senselessness of the fighting. One military man who studied with Morihei declared, "If we had really understood what Morihei was teaching us about entering and becoming one with an enemy, we would have never gotten involved in such a stupid war!" In 1942, Morihei resigned all his official positions, pleading serious illness, and he withdrew to his farm in Iwama, located about two hours from Tōkyō, where he and his wife lived in a little hut. Morihei cut all his ties to the world and devoted himself to the spiritual discipline he now called Aikidō.

In 1945, the war came to its disastrous conclusion, and Japan lay in ruins. Morihei, though, was optimistic. "Even if a country is defeated and its cities and industries destroyed," he told his few remaining students, "it still has its mountains and rivers." In other words, as long as the land remains intact, people can draw on their natural inner resources and recover from even the worst defeat. Morihei was confident that Aikidō—"divine techniques that do not kill"—would play an essential role in Japan's recovery and in the emerging world civilization.

Aikidō and all the other martial arts (with the exception of Karate) were banned by the U.S. occupation authorities. Even if those arts

Morihei in 1937, aged fifty-two, at his physical and technical peak. This painting was done by Rev. Takahashi, a Japanese Baptist minister. Morihei enjoyed associating with religious leaders of all persuasions.

Morihei, in his mid-sixties, clad in his favorite training outfit. After the war, Morihei assumed the countenance and bearing of a Taoist immortal.

While many postwar photos taken of Morihei show him smiling serenely, his glare could still be dreadful, as in this photograph shot in Wakayama in 1951 when he was sixty-seven years old. Morihei told his disciples, "If you ever catch me off guard, I'll present you with a teaching license." The disciples were constantly trying to do so, but whenever the thought crossed their minds, Morihei would suddenly glare at them like this.

had not been prohibited, in the aftermath of war there would have been very few trainees anyway, because everyone was too busy trying to survive and too hungry to expend precious energy moving around. Hidden in the countryside, Morihei did, however, manage to have a small group of disciples live and quietly train with him in Iwama in the immediate postwar years. Morihei's daily schedule in Iwama in those years was nearly ideal:

> 6:00 A.M.: Morning prayers and meditation in front of the outdoor Aiki Shrine.
> 7:00–9:00 A.M.: Aikidō training followed by a simple breakfast.
> 9:00 A.M.–noon: Farmwork.

12:00 A.M.–2:00 P.M.: Midday break for lunch and rest.
2:00–4:00 P.M.: Farmwork.
4:00–6:00 P.M.: Aikidō training.
6:00–7:00 P.M.: Bath.
7:00–8:30 P.M.: Evening prayers and meditation, followed by dinner.
8:30–9:30 P.M.: Students would massage Morihei's shoulders and legs, read to him, and chat with him before he retired for the evening.

Aikidō training resumed in earnest in Tōkyō around 1950, and over the following two decades the practice of Aikidō spread rapidly both in Japan and abroad. Under the direction of Morihei's son and eventual successor, Kisshōmaru, branch dōjō were quickly established over much of Japan. A number of Japanese instructors traveled overseas, some settling permanently, introducing Aikidō to the world at large. Foreign trainees also came to Japan to study, and when they returned home to their native countries to open their own dōjō, the Aikidō network expanded further. (There were some foreign trainees in the prewar period as well, mostly Italians, some Germans, and one or two professional American wrestlers, but their study was of short duration.)

In 1958, Morihei appeared in an episode of the U.S. television documentary series "Rendezvous with Adventure," and he was the star of a documentary film produced by a Japanese TV network in 1961.

In his final years, Morihei spent much of his time in prayer, meditation, and study, but he also traveled extensively (including a trip to Hawaii in 1961), deeply impressing a new crop of students with dazzling displays of Aikidō techniques and totally confounding them with his mysterious explanations of the secrets of the art. Even D. T. Suzuki, the great Zen scholar, confessed after hearing Morihei talk, "You know, I couldn't follow a thing you said."

Morihei training outdoors in front of the Aiki Shrine in Iwama. Morihei preferred to train outside, in nature, and even indoors he kept the windows wide open in all seasons.

True, Morihei spoke in a kind of "twilight language" that was deliberately obscure, but when his students complained that his style of speech was too old-fashioned for them to understand, Morihei would reply with a chuckle, "No, no, what I am saying is the very latest." Indeed, Morihei's teachings focused on all the concerns of today's New Age: the necessity of unifying mind and body; conflict resolution instead of confrontation; everyday life as an act of worship, as a celebration; maintenance of a healthy lifestyle; the importance of regular meditation; and concern for and care of the environment.

Morihei's health gradually declined, and in 1968 he began to suf-

Morihei bedecked with leis received upon his arrival in Hawaii in 1961. The founder was invited there for the grand opening of the Honolulu Aikikai Dōjō. Morihei told his students, "Hawaii is a wonderful place, but all the agricultural chemicals used here are destroying the islands. Try to stop this desecration of your land."

Morihei, eyes flashing and mouth wide open as he emits a devastating *kiai*, demonstrating Aikidō in Hawaii.

fer from liver cancer. Even on his deathbed, though, he was able to demonstrate miraculous power if someone treated him like a sick old man. Once he sent four attendants flying when they persisted in trying to assist when he did not need their help. Morihei died on April 26, 1969, at age 86. Among his final words was the declaration, "Aikidō is for the entire world."

Although Aikidō originated in Japan, it is now an integral part of world culture, practiced by people of many different nationalities in all parts of the globe. Morihei remains a living presence in most training halls, and his example continues to inspire each new generation of Aikidō students.

Morihei was quite secretive before the war regarding his techniques, but in his final years he opened up and enjoyed demonstrating the beauty, grace, and spirit of Aikidō to appreciative audiences such as this group, the Byakkō Prayer Society.

Morihei with his lifelong companion, Hatsu, in 1963. Morihei's disciples said of her: "She worked as hard as Ō-Sensei to make Aikidō a success." They were married sixty-six years, and after Morihei died in 1969 she joined him two months later to the day.

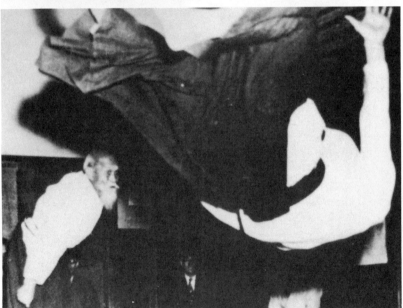

Even in his eighties, Morihei retained his incredible powers, able to hold three young men, pushing with all their might, at bay (*top*) or tossing one of his young disciples ten feet through the air (*bottom*).

Morihei, at age eighty-five, in front of the new Aikikai Hombu
Dōjō, which was completed in 1968, the year before his death.
Morihei told his students: "Aikidō has no limits. In Aikidō, the
entire world is our dōjō, and our training never ceases. The practice
of Aikidō is a lifelong task."

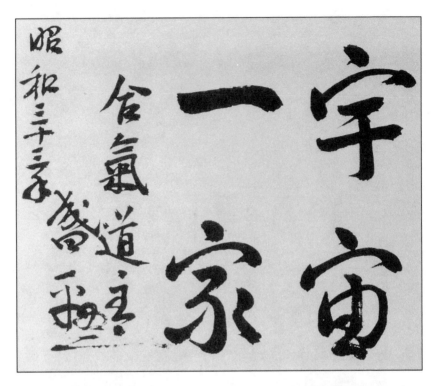

"The universe is one family," signed "Grandmaster of Aikidō, Morihei" and dated "Shōwa 33" (1958). On his deathbed, Morihei told his disciples, "Aikidō is for the entire world," and he encouraged them to spread the Art of Peace all over the globe.

2

The Art of Aikidō

THE PRINCIPLES of Aikidō need to be experienced through actual
practice. Training in Aikidō consists of preliminary exercises to warm
up the body and prepare the mind, paired exercises with a partner,
and work with the *bokken* (wooden sword) and *jō* (wooden staff).
The techniques include a variety of throws, locks, and pins (the martial art dimension); special exercises to foster physical and mental
power (the psychological dimension); and tactics of nonviolence and
harmonization (the spiritual dimension). In Aikidō, a sincere practitioner continually strives to forge the body, discipline the mind,
and polish the spirit.

The most distinctive characteristic of Aikidō, as conceived by its
founder, Morihei Ueshiba, is that there are no contests or organized
competitions. In Aikidō, the goal is to subdue one's base nature and
triumph over one's weaknesses or fears rather than to defeat an opponent in some trivial game. Morihei wrote in his manual, *Budō*:

> Sports are widely practiced nowadays, and they are good for
> physical exercise. Warriors, too, train the body, but they also
> use the body as a vehicle to train the mind, calm the spirit, and
> find goodness and beauty, dimensions that sports lack. Training
> in [Aikidō] fosters valor, sincerity, fidelity, magnanimity, and
> beauty, as well as making the body strong and healthy.

27

In Aikidō, partners take turns being the "attacker" and "defender," thus experiencing both sides of the "winner-loser" equation. Aikidō practitioners are instructed to work *with* each other, hand in hand, so that anyone who makes the effort will be able to cross the finish line. Training in Aikidō is sport, in the original meaning of that term: "to delight in physical activity, to play with exhilaration." Sport in its purest form has nothing to do with the final score.

There is an interesting story regarding the noncompetitive, defensive nature of Aikidō. After the war, Morihei refused to let any matches be held in the Hombu Dōjō, but once, for some reason, he relented and let Kōichi Tōhei, one of his top disciples, square off against a professional wrestler from South America. Usually such challengers rush right in and attack, but the wrestler held back. After some minutes of stalemate, the impatient Tōhei moved in and forced the issue, managing to get the wrestler down and pin him. Morihei, however, was quite displeased: "There is no need to throw someone who is not attacking you!" It seems that the wrestler had first visited the Kōdōkan Jūdō headquarters. There he was advised by the Jūdō people, "Don't attack an Aikidō man first; if you do, he will be sure to throw you."

This is not to say that Aikidō lacks an edge because it has no organized competition. Morihei described his style of training as *shi-ai*, "an encounter with death," which is the greatest challenge we will ever have to face. Aikidō practitioners are always dealing with techniques that have the potential to be lethal, and such training demands the utmost concentration and intensity.

Another distinctive feature of Aikidō is that everyone trains together: men and women, young and old, veteran and novice, big and little, heavy and light, flexible and stiff, aggressive and passive. By training with different partners, one learns to tailor the techniques to fit each individual situation. This shared experience enables one to build a solid foundation in the art of living as well—one learns how to deal with all kinds of people.

One can train forever in Aikidō. The pace of training and execution of the techniques can be adjusted as one grows older, and many people continue to practice Aikidō into ripe old age—the senior Aikidō instructor in Hawaii actively leads four classes a week at age ninety. Nor are there any physical barriers to the practice of Aikidō. I once had a student who was lacking a left arm, and another who was blind. The flexible techniques of Aikidō allowed both students to make the necessary adjustments, and they were able to train on an equal basis with the rest of the members of the dōjō.

Now let us turn to the fundamentals of Aikidō training.

Aikidō techniques are largely derived from the classical forms of Japanese martial arts, especially swordsmanship. To counter a sword attack, the unarmed warrior to the left applies a technique, a variation of which is still used in Aikidō today (called *gokyō*). Aikidō contains the best elements of Kendō, Jūdō, and Karate, for, as Morihei said, "Even though Aikidō is different from the martial arts of the past, it is not necessary to totally abandon the old ways. Absorb venerable traditions into Aikidō by clothing them with fresh garments, and build on the classic styles to create better forms."

Opposite, top: Rinjirō Shirata (1912–1993), one of Morihei's first and finest students, demonstrating the classical Aikidō *kamae* (stance). Morihei adapted this stance from traditional swordsmanship (*opposite, bottom*). In the martial arts it is often said that the most difficult thing to do is to really stand well in a good stance. In the old days, many a swordfight was decided as soon as the combatants assumed their stances—an experienced swordsman could tell instantly from his opponent's *kamae* if there would be an opportunity to attack. (If there was no hope for finding an opening in the opponent's defenses, a smart swordsman would withdraw.) After the basic stance has been mastered, it is possible to let the hands settle naturally toward the ground (*above*). Morihei taught, "A good stance reflects a proper state of mind," and the stance he displays here is centered and stable.

Both before (*top*) and after (*bottom*) the war, Morihei frequently explained Aikidō techniques in terms of sword movements.

A key element Morihei Ueshiba adopted from classical martial arts was *aiki* timing. *Aiki* timing enables one to completely unbalance an attacker, as demonstrated here by Morihei as he shifts ninety degrees to the inside and directs the blow down and to the front. (Photos from the Noma Dōjō series.)

The basic Aikidō training uniform (*left*), called in Japanese *dō-gi, keiko-gi,* or simply *gi,* is similar to that employed in Jūdō or Karate. The *hakama* skirt (*right*), once classical samurai dress, is also worn over the basic uniform. In some schools the *hakama* is worn by all trainees, but usually it is a privilege reserved for more advanced students who have displayed sufficient devotion to the art. Donning the appropriate uniform helps put one in the proper frame of mind for training.

Opposite: Two more examples of *aiki* timing: (*top*) Morihei steps in with triangular footwork to defuse an attack; (*bottom*) here Morihei opens to the side at a ninety-degree angle to neutralize the blow. Although there is no longer any practical reason to practice such seated techniques, Morihei considered *suwari-waza* essential for building up lower body strength and stability.

Above: Indoors, Aikidō is practiced in a dōjō, "the space of enlightenment." The dōjō floor is covered with *tatami* mats to facilitate rolling and to break falls, and the front wall (*shōmen*) is typically adorned with a calligraphic scroll (*kakejiku*) and a portrait of the founder of Aikidō, Morihei Ueshiba. A traditional Aikidō dōjō is kept as bright and uncluttered as possible, and it is swept thoroughly prior to and after training. Certain Aikidō movements require lots of open space, so Morihei also highly recommended outdoor training in Mother Nature's dōjō.

Opposite: Aikidō training always begins and ends with a bow, called *rei* in Japanese. Sitting on the floor, close to the ground, is a traditional sign of respect. Aikidō practitioners bow to the *shōmen* (*top*) to show their respect and gratitude for the teachings of Morihei; this is not an act of worship but a heartfelt thanks as well as a kind of salute. After bowing to the *shōmen*, the senior instructor and students bow to each other (*bottom*). The traditional greeting here is "Onegai-shimasu," "Let's help one another train." Training concludes with the same etiquette and a simple "Arigatō gozaimashita," "Thank you very much." These Japanese greetings may be replaced with similar sentiments expressed in one's own language, if desired.

Various warm-up exercises are employed in Aikidō. Morihei liked to use traditional exercises such as *uchi-gatame* ("softly pounding the body"), while other instructors utilize yoga or modern calisthenics. Regardless of the method, it is essential that the body be properly stretched and conditioned prior to actual training.

After the warm-up exercises to prepare one's body for Aikidō
training, there is usually some kind of meditation exercise to
prepare one's mind. Some of these meditation exercises can be
rather formal (see p. 82); others are more brief. The most
common short form of Aikidō meditation is known as *furi-tama*,
"shaking down the spirit." This is an exercise adopted from
Shintō *misogi* ritual. In *furi-tama*, the practitioner closes the
eyes, clasps the hands, and shakes them up and down vigorously
as he or she imagines the soul, fractured and dispersed by the
stress of daily life, becoming whole again and settling down into
the core of the practitioner's being. He or she will try to keep
the spirit centered there throughout the training.

Morihei teaching a class in the original Hombu Dōjō in Tōkyō around 1960. In Aikidō training, the instructor first demonstrates and explains a technique while the students observe; then they pair off and take turns practicing the technique until the instructor claps his or her hands and proceeds to the next technique.

Paired Aikidō training usually begins from a *katate-dori* ("held by one hand") position. This position facilitates bonding between the *nage* ("the one who throws") and the *uke* ("the one who receives"). An alternate term for *nage* is *tori* ("the one who takes" the decisive action). (In more direct terms, *nage* is the defender and *uke* is the attacker.) The *nage* (right) displays the classic posture (*kamae*) of Aikidō: triangular stance, straight spine, shoulders relaxed, arms extended, and fingers charged with *ki* (energy), gaze not fixed to any particular spot. The *uke* (left) is similarly alert yet relaxed, ready to receive the technique in a safe and appropriate manner. The techniques are always practiced alternately to the right and left, usually twice on each side, and then the positions of *nage* and *uke* are reversed. Medical studies have shown that equal use of both hands more evenly stimulates both sides of the brain, which helps keep logical and creative thinking in balance.

Other attacks commonly utilized in Aikidō training include (*a*) *shōmen-uchi* (direct attack to the head), delivered here by the practitioner on the right, and *yokomen-uchi* (attack to the side of the head or neck), delivered by the practitioner on the left (such attacks in Aikidō are delivered with the *tegatana*, or hand-sword, rather than a fist); (*b*) *tsuki* (punch/thrusts to the stomach or face); (*c*) *kata-dori* (shoulder grab); (*d*) *ryōte-dori* (held by both hands); (*e*) *morote-dori* (held by two hands on one arm); and (*f*) *ushiro-dori* (held from behind). At first, Aikidō attacks may appear to be stylized and comparatively tame, because the speed and force of an attack depends on the ability of the *nage* to handle it. Over the years, however, a practitioner gradually learns how to handle increasingly swift and powerful attacks. In classical Aikidō a strike or blow is accompanied by a *kiai*, a piercing shout, as illustrated in (*a*). Morihei never omitted *kiai* when training—his thundering *kiai* could be heard a mile away—but for some reason many schools have largely abandoned the use of *kiai* and some even discourage the practice, an unfortunate departure from Aikidō tradition.

a

b

c

d

e

f

Often in Aikidō training the principle of *yobi-dashi* ("calling out") is applied. As soon as the "attacker" to the left closes in, the "defender" to the right anticipates the attack and draws him out by shooting a *shōmen* blow to his head. This is a kind of preemptive strike, designed to disarm and control an attack before it has an opportunity to develop fully. Morihei frequently advised his students, "Rather than smashing your partner with brute force, defuse an attack by first leading and guiding it around you."

Even when one's partner initiates the attack, as shown here, an experienced Aikidō practitioner is able to read it instantly and move in to defuse it. The attacker has struck first, but Shirata Sensei is already the "winner" by positioning himself in the right place and by maintaining a powerful and ready stance.

A good *ukemi* (break-fall) allows an Aikidō practitioner to receive the countering move of the *nage* in a smooth and safe manner. Smashing one's partner to the mat is not acceptable behavior in Aikidō; instead the *uke* is permitted to take a natural break-fall to either the front (foreground) or to the back (rear). *Ukemi* take a bit of time to learn, but once mastered, such break-falls make Aikidō training safe and enjoyable.

Advanced practitioners are able to perform *tobu-ukemi*, "flying break-falls," flipping in the air yet still landing on the mat softly. Such break-falls can become second nature, and I had a student whose ability to execute *tobu-ukemi* saved his life. Late one night, while riding his motorcycle, he hit an unilluminated barrier on the road. He was thrown head over heels from his bike but managed to escape unharmed thanks to a spectacular *tobu-ukemi*.

Left: Various types of *atemi* (a blow directed to an anatomical weak point) have a place in Aikidō. In classical styles, the techniques are designed so it is possible to deliver an *atemi* at any juncture, as demonstrated here by Rinjirō Shirata against a *shōmen* strike, but such blows are used to defuse an attack, to unbalance one's partner, or to preclude a countermove, rather than to inflict a lethal blow. Some schools of Aikidō emphasize *atemi* more than others. *Above:* The *atemi* to the solar plexus (which will in training stop short of actual contact) is designed to break the force of the attack, enabling the *nage* to disarm the attacker and then apply a throw or pin.

a

Another singular feature of Aikidō is that one practices as if there are attacks coming from all directions. Thus, one cannot focus exclusively on one opponent; the Aikidō practitioner must always remain aware of potential attackers to the front and back (*a*) and to the sides. Such training fosters an open-mindness that is valuable both on the mat and in daily life—one learns how to keep the "big picture" always in view. In this illustration, the *nage* first gets out of the way of both attacks (*b*) and then puts himself in a safe place, keeping his partners in full view (*c*). This kind of training is also good for learning about *ma-ai*, proper spacing, between oneself and the direction and intensity of an attack.

b

c

Aikidō techniques are structured around six main pillars. The first pillar is *shihō-nage* ("four-directions throw"). This is a type of arm-throw taught in every Aikidō dōjō and usually practiced in some form at least once in every training session. Even though it is an elementary Aikidō technique, it is one of the most subtle. My teacher, Rinjirō Shirata, once remarked, "I've been practicing *shihō-nage* for fifty years and I still haven't gotten it down just right." *Shihō-nage* symbolizes the four gratitudes (toward the universe, toward our ancestors, toward our fellow human beings, and toward the plants and animals that provide us with food) and the four virtues of Aikidō (bravery, wisdom, love, and empathy).

Irimi (entering) is the second pillar of Aikidō. Technically, *irimi* involves entering deeply around or behind an attack to defuse it. *Irimi* is the technique of blending, of entering into an attack and becoming one with it, leaving the partner with nowhere to strike. In the *irimi-nage* illustrated here, the *nage* can bring the *uke* down with just a slight twist of the hips.

Perhaps the key movement in Aikidō is *kaiten* ("open and turn"), also known as *irimi-tenkan* ("enter and turn"). First one opens (or enters) to the side of an attack and then turns around it, completely defusing and neutralizing the force of the aggression. The exercise illustrated here will conclude with a *kote-gaeshi* (wrist-turn) throw. *Kaiten* movements are circular and free-flowing, the image that first comes to mind when one thinks of Aikidō. *Kaiten* movements symbolize the freedom and adaptability of Aikidō, and Morihei once stated, "The secret of *kaiten* movements lies in your mind, not your body!"

Opposite: Kokyū (breath) techniques have two aspects. The first is *kokyū-hō* (breath-power training), a special set of exercises that build power based on the life force rather than on brute strength. The notion of *kokyū* is akin to *prāṇa*, the Sanskrit term for "all-pervading breath of the universe." In *kokyū-hō*, the Aikidō practitioner attempts to plug into that universal flow of breath. Most Aikidō training sessions conclude with the *suwari* (seated) *kokyū-hō* technique shown here (*top*). Sometimes *kokyū-hō* is practiced while being held by two (or more) partners to increase the level of difficulty (*bottom*).

The second aspect of *kokyū* is timing, the ability to read an attack and apply the technique at just the right instant. While *kokyū-hō* is set and static, *kokyū* timing is dynamic. *Kokyū* represents the sustaining power of life and the good timing we need to negotiate our way through life.

Osae-waza are the locks and pins of Aikidō. When properly applied, Aikidō locks and pins stimulate and greatly strengthen the muscles and joints of the shoulder, arm, and wrist. (Applied improperly, such techniques will wreak havoc on the body.) These techniques are to be executed slowly and with no more force than necessary; nevertheless, there is no escaping the fact that the locks and pins of Aikidō are quite painful in the beginning. Forbearance is required, but eventually the joints will become supple and strong. *Osae-waza* symbolize control: control of the situation and control of oneself.

Ushiro-waza ("rear techniques") are designed to assist an Aikidō practitioner to refine his or her "sixth sense." In a real situation, you would never want to let someone get behind you, but in these techniques Aikidō practitioners allow their partners to do so to test their intuition and ability to respond without being able to see the attack. *Ushiro* techniques represent the intuition, presence of mind, and good judgment we need to function well in life.

Randori (free-style) techniques against simulated attacks by two or more partners are often practiced in Aikidō. Such training helps develop free-flowing movements, keen peripheral vision, quick reactions, and firm presence of mind. Good *zanshin*, remaining alert and on guard even after the technique is executed, is also vital in Aikidō training.

Numerous Aikidō techniques have practical application as a means of self-defense; demonstrated here is a technique to counter a knife attack to the neck. (This is a variation of the *jūjutsu* technique shown on p. 45.) This emphasis on self-defense varies from dōjō to dōjō (in some schools they train as if they expect to be in a street fight as soon as they walk out the door), but because the primary purpose of Aikidō is lifelong physical and spiritual development, self-defense should not be the principal reason for taking up the art. (If self-defense is the priority, then you should take a course specifically designed for that purpose.) Many people come to Aikidō with extensive experience in such deadly arts as kick-boxing, full-contact Karate, or military hand-to-hand combat, so they already know how to inflict mayhem. What they are looking for in Aikidō is something less violent and confrontational yet still effective. Most women also find Aikidō to be naturally effective as self-defense, because they are taught from the beginning to rely on keen awareness, good judgment, and evasive moves, rather than physical power, when confronted with a threat.

There are two schools of thought regarding Aikidō and children. Some instructors feel that because of the difficulty of the techniques and the complexity of the philosophy, Aikidō is not really suitable for children. It is better to let youngsters train in, for example, Karate and Jūdō, letting them come to Aikidō when they are more physically and emotionally mature. Instructors who are comfortable with children and accustomed to working with them, however, usually have good success adapting Aikidō for youngsters. It all depends on the inclination of the individual instructor.

a

In addition to body techniques (*tai-jutsu*), Aikidō includes training in the sword (*aiki-ken*) and the staff (*aiki-jō*). The sword (*a*) is used singly to improve body movements and strengthen the arms and grip in cutting practice (*suburi*); (*b*) in paired practice (*kumi-tachi*), the relationship between the sword movements and body techniques is explored; (*c*) in *tachi-dori* ("sword taking"), one learns how to utilize the "sword of no-sword" by facing an armed attack empty-handed. Sword movements largely define the body techniques of Aikidō.

b

c

a

The *jō* is also used individually (*a*), and (*b*) for partner practice (*kumi-jō*). On occasion, the *jō* is paired against the *ken* (*c*). Training with the *jō* fosters intuition and helps develop the ability to move freely and fluidly.

b

c

Suburi with either the sword or staff can be done in a group. During intensive training sessions, it is customary to do hundreds, even thousands, of cuts or thrusts with the *ken* and *jō*.

Morihei joyfully training with his students. A good instructor
employs a "hands-on" approach with his (or her) students,
often serving as the *uke* to help a beginner get the hang of a
technique. There is a wonderful film showing Morihei, the
grand master himself, taking a break-fall for one of his
elementary school trainees.

Regarding technique, Morihei taught: "In Aikidō, execution of the techniques should be as natural as walking, so skillful that they look effortless and prearranged."

Morihei told his students that Aikidō must always be practiced in "a vibrant and joyful manner." The atmosphere in a good Aikidō dōjō is typically bright, open, and friendly, and proper training generates light (wisdom), warmth (compassion), and energy (true strength).

It is a good idea to conclude training with another short period of meditation, either sitting or standing, both to cool down the body and to calm the mind. In Europe, I have seen many statues in churches displaying exactly the same posture illustrated here.

Parallels to the stances and movements of Aikidō are found in religious art all
over the world. The posture displayed midway through the execution of *kaiten-
nage* (*left*) reflects the dynamic stance of a Guardian King placed at the
entrance of a Japanese Buddhist temple (*right*). Careful observation of the
classical art of East and West can be a valuable resource for the practice of
Aikidō.

Morihei lectures on the philosophy of Aikidō to his students. In his final years,
the Founder spent much of each training session explaining the spiritual
significance of Aikidō, and he insisted: "Aikidō is the study of the spirit." It is
imperative to expend as much effort studying the profound philosophy of
Aikidō as practicing the techniques.

3

The Philosophy of Aikidō

Aɪᴋɪᴅō ɪs much more than a martial art. The Founder told his disciples: "Do you think I'm teaching you merely how to twist someone's arm and knock him to the ground? That's child's play. Aikidō deals with the most important issues of life!"

In the following section, the main tenets of Aikidō philosophy are outlined and illustrated. Many of the principles of Aikidō apply to all aspects of daily life. Aikidō is not simply a matter of physical technique; it is the art of living well, in harmony with others and at peace with the world. Morihei told his students:

> The wise warrior can freely utilize all elements contained in heaven and earth. A real warrior correctly perceives the essence of things, and learns how to transform techniques into vehicles of purity, goodness, and beauty. A true warrior manifests enlightened wisdom and deep calm.

Deep learning has always been an essential element of the samurai tradition, but no one stressed the importance of continual study more than Morihei. The Founder himself was always poring over sacred texts and their commentaries, and he encouraged his disciples to immerse themselves in the classics of East and West. Deep learning is defined as "possessing a rich knowledge of heaven and earth," and Morihei wanted his students to become cultured men and women familiar with all the sciences: philosophy, religion, art, music, literature, agriculture, physics, and mathematics.

Many Aikidō schools have a special name for their dōjō, usually ending with the character KAN, which means academy or hall of learning. This is the *gaku* (signboard) for the Kōdōkan. "The Path of Light Academy," brushed by Rinjirō Shirata. Morihei often referred to Aikidō as a "path of light," and in Aikidō schools, students strive to illumine various aspects of their tradition. *Keiko,* "using ancient wisdom to illuminate the present," is the traditional term used for regular training; *shugyō,* "intensive effort," is the term employed for more concentrated practice over a period of time; and *tanren,* "forging," is the term applied to rigorous, repeated exercises such as continuous cuts with the sword.

A study break during an intensive training session. In addition to individual study, group study in the dōjō is also valuable. Aikidō practitioners study the teachings of the Founder as expressed in his talks, poems, and calligraphy and then discuss the relevance of Aikidō philosophy to daily living in the modern world. The instructor also speaks of his (or her) own experiences and transmits the teachings of Aikidō in a personal, face-to-face, heart-to-heart manner. (Morihei's teachings are presented in depth in these books: *Budō: Teachings of the Founder of Aikidō; The Essence of Aikidō: Spiritual Teachings of Morihei Ueshiba; The Secrets of Aikidō;* and *The Art of Peace.* See Resources for detailed information.)

Morihei was often described as the "most religious person in Japan," and every morning and evening he would offer his prayers to Aiki Ō-Kami, "The Great Spirit of Aiki." Morihei taught that every human being is a "living shrine of the divine" and that all of us have the potential to become a buddha. Aikidō is not a religion, but practice of its principles helps us fathom the essence of religion and philosophy. Morihei intended Aikidō to be a type of yoga that linked the outer, inner, and spiritual realms of existence. (There are many parallels between Yoga and Aikidō. An Ayurvedic physician in Nepal who felt the pulse of one of my Aikidō students said to him, "I can tell that you have been practicing some kind of Yoga for a long time.")

The formal Aikidō bow (*rei*), made at the beginning and end of class, represents humility, respect, and gratitude. We humbly bow all the way to the ground, hands placed in a triangle, to show our respect for the tradition, and our hearts should be full of gratitude for the opportunity to practice. Such etiquette helps put Aikidō practitioners in the right frame of mind.

A bow can also serve as an Aikidō technique, as demonstrated here by Morihei. When our partner rushes in, we can "greet" him with a bow. (Many Aikidō warm-up exercises have practical application as techniques.) Once, a rival martial artist visited the Kobukan with a secret plan to attack Morihei as soon as the Aikidō master bowed down in greeting. Morihei's disciples were quite surprised when their teacher, who was usually very courteous, refused to bow to the visitor. The visitor stayed with his head down for some time before Morihei returned his bow. Later, the visitor confessed, "I planned to leap at him as soon as he returned my bow but when he didn't move, I realized that he had read my mind and defeated me. I stayed down in abject apology. Morihei read my mind again, and then bowed to indicate his forgiveness. He is a true master."

As in any other spiritual discipline, meditation plays an important role in Aikidō. During Aikidō *chinkon-kishin* ("calm the spirit and return to the source") meditation, Morihei advised: "Sit comfortably and then breathe in, letting yourself soar to the ends of the universe; breathe out and bring the cosmos back inside. This is the Breath of Heaven. Next, breathe up all the fecundity and vibrancy of the earth, and then breathe down to the ground. This is the Breath of Earth. Then blend the Breath of Heaven and the Breath of Earth with your own natural breathing, becoming the Breath of Life itself. Find your center, and settle in the heart of things. Keep your mind like the vast sky, the highest peak, and the deepest ocean." Reposing like this in *seiza* ("quiet and correct sitting") helps a practitioner divine the universal truths of "The Great Spirit of Aiki." *Kototama* chanting (refer to *Kototama: The Secret Sounds of Aikidō*; see Resources) is another valuable vehicle for calming the spirit and returning to the source. While Aikidō is often identified with Zen, it should be noted that the meditation techniques and general world-view of Aikidō are much closer to Tantra. (Calligraphy of Aiki Ō-Kami by the author.)

Sometimes just the simple act of greeting the rising sun at dawn can be a powerful form of *chinkon-kishin*. Morihei composed this verse:

> The morning sun
> floods my heart with light.
> From my doorway
> I soar to heaven
> bathed in divine radiance.

AI-KI-DŌ ("The Way of Harmony"), brushed by Morihei and hung as a scroll in the Hombu Dōjō in Tōkyō. As mentioned, *aiki* (blending and harmonization of energies) is a key concept in Asian philosophy, but Morihei expanded the meaning: "Aiki is the universal principle that brings all things together; it is the optimal process of harmonization that operates in all realms, from the vastness of space to the tiniest atoms." *Aiki* further signifies the unity of heaven, earth, and humankind, the ideal that inspires people to live in harmony with the environment and with each other. *Aiki* is mutual accord, the art of reconciliation, a virtue essential for civilized living. On an individual level, *aiki* stands for integration of body and spirit, a state of wholeness and balance. *Aiki* also represents the subtle power of nature: "Aiki can be a gentle breeze rustling the leaves, or the violent wind snapping large branches." *Dō* is both the particular "path" of Aikidō—actual practice of the physical and spiritual techniques—and a universal "way"—application of *aiki* principles to the world at large.

The bodies of both *nage* and *uke* bristle with *ki* in this Aikidō technique. *Ki* (*ch'i* in Chinese) is the life force of the universe, the active agent of creation. *Ki* is the universal energy that makes the world function: "Strength resides where one's *ki* is concentrated and stable; confusion and maliciousness reign when *ki* stagnates." Aikidō training fosters this vital force by helping practitioners focus their *ki*, circulate it through the body, and then extend it into the techniques. Also, when one's *ki* is circulating well, one is healthy and vital.

Sometimes the flow of *ki* in Aikidō techniques is more relaxed and circular, centered in the belly, as shown here. It is important for the *uke*, too, to follow the flow of energy, thus creating a natural *aiki* circuit.

Ki also means spirited, and here we see a female *jūjutsu* master named Matsumoto Ai thrashing four would-be rapists. *Ki* power can be summoned up equally well by women, and no woman should be afraid of standing up to protect herself from physical or emotional abuse. Woodblock print by Yoshitoshi (1839–1892).

Another aspect of *ki* is *kiai*, the "shout of life." A good *kiai* is like the cry of a newborn baby, and *naga-iki*, "long life," is synonymous with "long breath." Shirata Sensei's *kiai* was particularly powerful, filling the dōjō with charged energy.

a   b

Bushin, "Martial Spirit," brushed by Morihei (*a*) and his disciple Rinjirō Shirata (*b*). Aikidō is the progression from *bujutsu* (martial art) to *budō* (martial way) to *bushin* (martial spirit), the highest level of training. Although the calligraphy represents the same forms, the character of each of the two men is clearly reflected in their brushstrokes. Aikidō is not meant to make you a carbon copy of your teacher; it is meant to bring out your inner treasures.

Misogi means "purification," and both Shintō and Buddhist practitioners traditionally conducted *misogi* rituals in the ocean, in fast-flowing streams, or beneath waterfalls (*above*). Morihei liked to do such waterfall *misogi*, but he came to consider the practice of Aikidō itself to be the best kind of *misogi*. Indeed, after a good training session in Aikidō, one often feels refreshed and restored.

Misogi performed with a *jō* in the courtyard of a medieval European church. The concept of *misogi* is somewhat akin to the notion of baptism in Christianity, that is, "a return to a state of unadorned purity." There is a *misogi* of the body (washing away of dirt), a *misogi* of the mind (cleansing oneself of defiling thoughts), and a *misogi* of the environment (keeping one's immediate space neat and well ordered). The purpose of *misogi* is "to make the world continually afresh, to create each day anew." Prior to each training session, Morihei would perform *misogi-no-jō* to purify his mind and body.

TAKE-MU-SU AI-KI ("Courageous and Creative Living"),
brushed by Rinjirō Shirata. Morihei frequently summarized
his teaching as *takemusu aiki*. The primary meaning of *take*
(also pronounced "bu" as in "Budō") is "martial," but in
Aikidō the term signifies courage, bravery, valor, and chivalry.
Take also symbolizes commitment—the commitment to
train hard, the commitment to overcome all obstacles, the
commitment to follow the path of Aiki to the end. *Musu* is
birth, the creation of life, fecundity. In Aikidō, *musu* means
to continually create fresh techniques of harmonization that
link things together. When *take* and *musu* are bound by *aiki*,
it is possible to live with courage, conviction, and creativity.

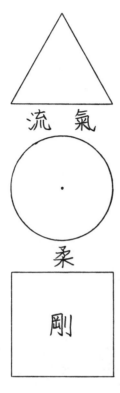

流　氣

柔

剛

Morihei often remarked, "The only way I can really explain Aikidō is by means of the triangle, circle, and square." The triangle represents *ki* and *ryū*, the generation and flow of energy, and it symbolizes the various trinities of existence: heaven, earth, and humankind; body, mind, and spirit; man, woman, and child; birth, maturity, and death; truth, goodness, and beauty. Technically, the triangle represents the stable triangular stance of Aikidō, initiative, and entering. The circle stands for the principle of *jū*, flexibility and suppleness. A circle with a dot in the center symbolizes perfect resolution, harmony of all powers, and continual revolution. Physically, circular movements are the key to blending with a partner, the source of unlimited techniques. The square represents *kon*, the diamond element: solid, stable, real, and well proportioned. The square is the basis of the total control necessary for the proper performance of Aikidō techniques.

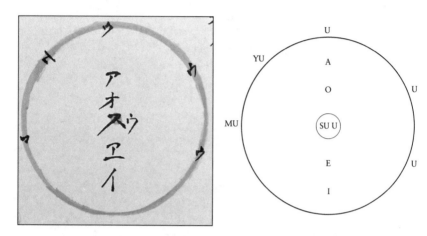

Morihei's mandala of the Aiki cosmos (*left*), with English translation (*right*).
In the center is SU, the seed syllable of the universe. From this explosive center the primordial sounds A (=heaven)—O (=earth)—U (=link together)—
E (=water)—I (=fire) and U-U-U (=continual birth)—YU (=form)—
MU (=emptiness) emerge simultaneously, creating the world through *aiki* in-
teraction. Morihei based much of his philosophy on the science of *kototama*,
"word-spirit," an esoteric body of knowledge that is present, in some form, in
all cultures. *Kototama* is the most difficult aspect of Aikidō philosophy, and it
takes years of experience and study to grasp the reality of these sounds of the
spirit. (Detailed explanations of Morihei's *kototama* teachings are given in *The
Essence of Aikidō: Spiritual Teachings of Morihei Ueshiba* and *The Secrets of
Aikidō;* see Resources.)

Left: Ame-no-murakumo kuki samuhara ryū-ō, brushed by Rinjirō Shirata. This is the title of an esoteric deity, Morihei's guardian angel, and a code name for the secret teaching of Aikidō. *Ame-no-murakumo,* "billowing clouds of heaven," symbolizes the churning of creation; *kuki,* "nine fierce spirits," represents the dynamic energy that sustains that creation; *samuhara,* "cold and clear plain," stands for insight into the true nature of that creation; *ryū-ō,* "dragon-king," idealizes a human being who soars beyond the material and approaches the spiritual. *Right:* Pictorial representation of *Ame-no-murakumo kuki samuhara ryū-ō* placed in the alcove of the old Hombu Dōjō.

Left: *Masakatsu Agatsu* ("True victory is self victory") and (*right*) *Katsuhayabi-no-waza* ("The techniques of victory right here, right now"), brushed by Morihei: " 'True victory' means unflinching courage; 'self-victory' symbolizes unflagging effort; and 'victory right here, right now!' represents the glorious moment of triumph in the here and now. The techniques of *katsuhayabi* are free of set forms, enabling one to respond immediately to any contingency. Those who are enlightened to these principles are always victorious. Winning without contending is true victory, a victory over oneself, a victory swift and sure."

Tenchi-nage, "heaven-and-earth throw." Just as heavens and earth separate when the universe is created, the hands part when this technique is initiated, one hand extending up toward the sky, and one hand reaching down toward the ground. By practicing Aikidō techniques, one learns to appreciate the subtle philosophy implicit in all aspects of the art.

Morihei stressed that Aikidō techniques must always be "true," "good," and "beautiful." *True* means well executed and effective; *good* means not to inflict injury; and *beautiful* means to perform the techniques gracefully with as much style and sensitivity as an artist, as illustrated here. Aikidō techniques must also reflect the natural rhythm of the universe: (*opposite*) "Look at the way a stream wends its way through a mountain valley, smoothly transforming itself as it flows over and around the rocks."

SELECTED TEACHINGS OF MORIHEI UESHIBA

The universe is our greatest teacher, our greatest friend. Look at the way a stream wends its way through a mountain valley, smoothly transforming itself as it flows over and around the rocks. The world's wisdom is contained in books, and by studying them, countless new techniques can be created. Study and practice, and then reflect on your progress. Aikidō is the art of learning deeply, the art of knowing oneself.

———

Aiki is an inexhaustible fount of wisdom. It is the source of all the true knowledge contained in the world's classics. But *aiki* is not something you can master in four or five years. It takes at least ten years to grasp the basics of *aiki,* and it is dangerous to foolishly strive for some grandiose experience that you think will render you instantly enlightened. Never consider yourself an all-knowing master. You must always be training and studying with your students.

———

In Aikidō we learn about ourselves, we learn to link ourselves to the life force, and we learn how to discern the principles of nature. Step by step, we make our path one of brightness and peace.

———

The universe itself is always teaching us Aikidō, but we fail to perceive it. Everyone thinks only of him- or herself, and that is why there is so much contention and discord in our world. If we could just keep our hearts pure, everything would be fine. Do not think that the divine exists high above us in heaven. The divine is right here, within and around us. The purpose of Aikidō is to remind us that we are always in a state of grace.

———

The practice of Aikidō is an act of faith, a belief in the power of nonviolence. It is not a type of rigid discipline or empty asceticism. It is a path that follows the principles of nature, principles that must apply to daily living. Aikidō should be practiced from the time you rise to greet the morning to the time you retire at night.

———

Aikidō is nonviolence. Every human being has been entrusted with a mandate from heaven, and the victory we seek is to overcome all challenges and fight to the finish, accomplishing our goals. In Aikidō we never attack. If you want to strike first, to gain advantage over someone, that is proof your training is insufficient, and it is really you yourself who has been defeated. Let your partner attack, and use his aggression against him. Do not cower from an attack; control it before it begins. Nonviolence is the true practice of Aikidō.

———

In my Aikidō, there are no opponents, no enemies. I do not want to overwhelm everyone with brute strength, nor do I want to smash every challenger to the ground. In true *budō* there are no opponents, no enemies. In true *budō* we seek to be one with all things, to return to the very heart of creation. The purpose of Aikidō training is not to make you simply stronger or tougher than others; it is to make you a warrior for world peace. This is our mission in Aikidō.

———

Many paths lead to the peak of Mount Fuji, but the goal is the same. There are many methods of reaching the top, but they all can bring us to the heights. There is no need to battle with each other—we are all brothers and sisters who should walk the path together, hand in hand. Keep to the path, and nothing else will matter. When you lose your desire for things that do not matter, you will be free. Those who desire nothing possess everything.

———

We can no longer totally rely on the external teachings of Buddha, Confucius, or Christ. The era of organized religion controlling every aspect of life is over. No single religion has all the answers. Each one of us is inherently a god or goddess. Cooperate with all the myriad deities of this world, and fulfill your duty as a messenger of the divine.

———

All things are really One, and past, present, and future are contained in each breath we take. The subtle nature of human existence contains the entire truth. The universe has come into being from a Single Source, and we ourselves are an essential element of that continual evolution, the optimal process of harmonization.

———

Aiki, the art of harmonization, is the key. When one's *ki* is circulating freely, sickness does not arise. We want to cure the world of the sickness of violence, malcontent, and discord—this is the Path of Aiki. Let go of petty thoughts and selfish desires, and you can live in true freedom.

———

Life is a divine gift. The divine is not something outside of us; it is right in our very center, it is our freedom. In the dōjō we are always learning about life and death. To be victorious is to create life; to be defeated is to give up and die. Abandon petty thoughts, empty yourself, transcend life and death, and stand upright in the center of vast creation. This is the secret of Aikidō.

———

We constantly need to purify our senses. Our sense organs allow us to function in this world, but as soon as they are disturbed or agitated, we lose our bearings. This causes confusion and disorder in the world, and that is the worst sin of all. Continually polish your spirit, keep your senses fresh and bright, and you will bring light to this world.

————

First of all, you must put your own life in order. Then you must learn how to maintain ideal relations within your own family. After that, you must work to improve the conditions in your own country, and then how to live harmoniously with the world at large. This is our duty as practitioners of Aikidō.

————

Aiki is the process of eliminating enmity and discord. Aikidō is the discipline of perceiving the true nature of the cosmos. Enter right into the heart of things, make that your base, and open your own door to truth. Create a universe within, and remain in tune with the universe at large.

————

The heart of the universe is no different from one's own heart. What is the heart of the universe? It contains the poles of existence, the four directions, past and present, all there is—it is universal love. Love does not fight. Love has no enemies. If your mind harbors enmity and hatred, you have lost the universal mind.

————

In real *budō* there are no enemies. Real *budō* is the function of love. The Way of a Warrior is not to destroy and kill but to foster life, to continually create. Love is the divinity that can really protect us.

Without love, nothing can flourish. Aikidō is the manifestation of love.

―――――

Economy is the basis of society. When the economy is stable, society can develop. The best economic policy is to create products with both material and spiritual value. Sell "sincerity" and "love" and you can never go wrong. In Aikidō, too, we offer "caring," a product that invariably attracts people.

―――――

Keep your hands, hips, and feet in a straight line and your body and mind centered. Your hands are the key to systematically guiding and controlling your partner. If your partner pulls, let him pull, but become one with that pull yourself. In training, discern that which the opponent lacks and then supply it. That is Aikidō.

―――――

In good Aikidō training, we generate light (wisdom) and heat (compassion). Those two elements activate heaven and earth, the sun and the moon; they are the subtle functions of water and fire. When the universal truth of *kototama* is manifest, we will be able to find the right path for us to follow. Unify the material and spiritual realms, and that will enable you to become truly brave, wise, loving, and empathetic.

―――――

In order to practice Aikidō properly, you must not forget that all things originate from One Source; envelop yourself with love, and embrace sincerity. A technique that is based only on physical force is weak; a technique based on spiritual power is strong.

―――――

War must cease. We are all members of one big family; now is the time to eliminate fighting and contention. This world was created to be a thing of beauty. If there is no love between us, that will be the end of our home, the end of our country, and the end of our world. Love generates heat and light. That is the spirit of Aikidō training.

———

Aikidō is good for the health. It helps you manifest your inner and outer beauty. It fosters good manners and proper deportment. Aikidō teaches you how to respect others, and how not to behave in a rude manner. It is not easy to live up to the ideals of Aikidō but we must do so at all costs—otherwise our training is in vain.

———

Keep your mind circular, and your body triangular. Lose yourself in the deep mountains and quiet valleys and bind yourself to the life-generating *ki* of yin and yang. In such an *aiki* state, you can accomplish anything, even the most difficult task. If you are settled deep within yourself, nothing in daily life will be able to shackle you.

———

Keep your movement circular. Imagine a circle with a cross drawn through it. Place yourself in the center of that circle and stand there firmly in a triangular stance. Link yourself to the *ki* of heaven and earth, pivot around the front foot, and lead your partner around that center.

———

In the old days, a swordsman would let an enemy slice the surface of his skin in order to cut into his enemy's flesh; sometimes he would even sacrifice his flesh in order to slash through to the enemy's bone. In Aikidō, such an attitude is unacceptable. We want both attacker and defender to escape unharmed. Rather than risk injury to attain victory, you must learn how to lead your partner. Control an opponent by always putting yourself in a secure, safe place.

———

The hand-sword utilized in the body techniques is the hand-sword of heaven and earth. Envelop your partner with your mind, flood him with *ki*, and you will be able to instantly perceive his actions and respond appropriately. Envelop him with your mind and lead him along the path revealed to you by heaven and earth. Let him strike and then harmonize with the attack. Transcend life and death, and then you will be able to perceive clearly the path that will lead you safely through death and destruction.

———

There is no place in Aikidō for pettiness and selfish thoughts. Rather than being captivated by notions of "winning or losing," seek the true nature of things. Your thoughts should reflect the grandeur of the universe, a realm beyond life and death. If your thoughts are antagonistic toward the cosmos, those thoughts will destroy you and wreak havoc on the environment.

———

Masakatsu ("true victory") is associated with the male element of creation; *agatsu* ("self-victory") is associated with the female element; joined together harmoniously, they represent *katsuhayabi* ("victory right here, right now!"), an ideal state of perfection and completion.

———

You may possess miraculous powers, but if you are not practicing what you preach by working for world peace, your powers are meaningless. In Aikidō we make each day anew, shed old garments, and continue to advance, looking for the ties that bind heaven, earth, and humankind, and the manifest, hidden, and divine.

———

Train hard, experience the light and warmth of Aikidō, and be a real person. Train more, and learn the principles of nature. Aikidō is becoming established all over, but it will have a different expression in each place it takes root. Continually adapt the teachings and create a beautiful, pure land.

4

Schools and Styles of Aikidō

Morihei was a great visionary, but he left the practical details of organization to his followers, and his disciples branched out on their own, creating schools and styles based on their personal understanding of Aikidō. Aikidō dōjō, even the most eclectic, are nearly always grounded in one particular tradition, so it is helpful for a beginning student to know a bit about the background of prevalent Aikidō styles.

Prior to discussing the styles and schools of Aikidō, mention should be made of the Aikidō ranking system, because most instructors present themselves as being "such-and-such" *dan. Kyū* are the preliminary levels of training (in Japan, testing begins at the fifth *kyū*), and *dan* are the "black belt" ranks, beginning with *shodan* (first degree). *Nidan* (second degree) and *sandan* (third degree) indicate a certain level of technical competence and experience in the art, at the initial instructor level. *Yodan* (fourth degree) and *godan* (fifth degree) are meant to be advanced ranks akin to the titles, respectively, of assistant professor and associate professor in a university. *Rokudan* (sixth rank) confers the title of *shihan* ("senior instructor"), equivalent to the status of full professor. The highest ranks, *nanadan* (seventh), *hachidan* (eighth), *kyūdan* (ninth), and the ultimate *jūdan* (tenth) are reserved for those of outstanding achievement and long service to Aikidō. (Within the Aikikai—see below—the

Morihei established Aikidō and pointed us in the right direction, but it is up to us to follow that path and discover our own way, in our own idiom.

founder, Morihei Ueshiba, and his successors as *dōshu*, or grandmaster, assume a position outside the ranking system.)

Morihei adopted this ranking system from Jūdō and Kendō, but when he was alive he awarded *dan* rankings in a rather haphazard, even cavalier, fashion. He would, for example, suddenly jump a student two levels in rank before a public demonstration or verbally award a high honorary rank to a senior disciple if he happened to be in a good mood. The various schools that formed following Morihei's death established more formal criteria for promotion and instituted regular testing and evaluation procedures. However, these schemes do not really work well for a variety of reasons: some testing requirements are far more lenient than others (in Japan, for instance, it is possible to obtain *shodan* in one year, whereas overseas it usually requires five); favored students tend to pass through the ranks more quickly, while others are held back (often unreasonably); and the promise of a higher rank is used as an enticement to lure people from one organization to another. Another ploy is to form an organization of one's colleagues and have them issue the desired rank. Some have even dispensed with that charade, awarding themselves eighth, ninth, or tenth *dan*, typically justifying the act by announcing that Morihei appeared to them in a dream or vision and presented them with the exalted rank. On the other end of the spectrum, there are many fine Aikidō instructors who out of sincere humility have never sought high rank, focusing on training instead.

In short, an instructor should never be evaluated purely in terms of his or her *dan* ranking. Those rankings are essentially meaningless—a number of Aikidō practitioners today, in fact, advocate the abandoning of any type of ranking system—and the best instructors follow the dictum: Let your reputation be your rank.

Although the majority of Aikidō instructors are excellent teachers and fine individuals, there have been cases of instructors who have seriously compromised the ideals of Aikidō and totally violated its ethics. Physical or sexual abuse, on or off the mat, should never be tolerated from any instructor, no matter how senior, and students should expect (and demand) only the most professional behavior from their teachers. Here the guiding principle is: How you act is far more telling than what you say.

A final word on instructors. During the course of training, especially if one has occasion to train in several different styles, one is likely to encounter instructors who insist, "What you are doing is all wrong. This is the right way." This extremely shortsighted view displays an appalling ignorance of Aikidō tradition. Over the years, Morihei taught Aikidō differently to different people, and he often proclaimed, "Today's techniques will be different tomorrow!" Techniques change, instructors have different perspectives, and practitioners should share their experiences rather than argue over petty details—this is what Aikidō is all about. Rather than "That is wrong, this is right," Morihei taught: "If your heart is true and set on Aikidō, then—and only then—will you be performing the techniques correctly."

For further advice on how to select an Aikidō dōjō, see Susan Perry's excellent article, "How To Find an Aikidō Dōjō," in *Aikidō Today Magazine #24* (Vol. 6, No. 4, Oct/Nov 1992, pp. 36–40). Perry has also written an informative article on North American Aikidō organizations, including contact addresses and telephone numbers, called "American Aikidō Organizations" (*Aikidō Today Magazine #28*, Vol. 7, No. 2, June/July 1993, pp. 13–16). See "Resources" for ordering information.

THE PRINCIPAL WORLDWIDE SCHOOLS OF AIKIDŌ

Aikikai.   This is the largest and most "mainstream" Aikidō organization, headed by Kisshōmaru Ueshiba (b. 1921), Morihei's son, and headquartered in Tōkyō at the Hombu Dōjō, which is directed by Moriteru Ueshiba (b. 1951), Morihei's grandson. The Aikikai's International Aikidō Federation oversees the organization's global operations. Within the Aikikai itself there are several distinctive styles: Hombu-style Aikidō is characterized by the free-flowing, fast movements favored by Kisshōmaru and Moriteru Ueshiba. Classical Aikidō, inspired by the example of Rinjirō Shirata (1912–1993), encompasses the entire spectrum of Aikidō techniques and stresses the primacy of deep learning and spiritual refinement. Iwama-style Aikidō, taught by Morihiro Saitō (b. 1928), makes extensive use of *aiki-ken* and *aiki-jō* while placing great, even obsessive, emphasis on technique. Nishio-style Aikidō is a composite system devised by Shoji Nishio (b. 1927), who focuses on the relationship between Aikidō and *iai-dō* (swordsmanship), Karate, and *Budō* in general. Other Aikikai *shihan*, with distinctive styles and substantial followings at home and abroad, include Seiseki Abe (b. 1915), Shigenobu Okumura (b. 1922), Michio Hikitsuchi (b. 1923), Seigō Yamaguchi (b. 1924), Hiroshi Tada (b. 1929), Hirokazu Kobayashi (b. 1929) of

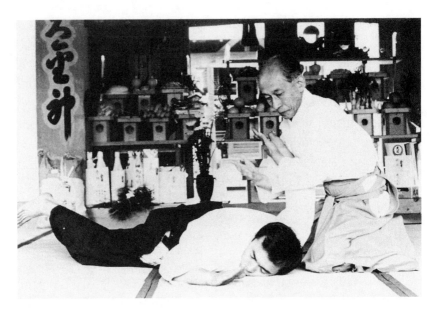

Dōshu Kisshōmaru Ueshiba, Morihei's son and present director of the Aikikai, performing a memorial demonstration at the Aiki Shrine in Iwama. An annual service in memory of Morihei is conducted there every April 29.

Ōsaka, Yasuo Kobayashi (b. 1936) of Tōkyō, Nobuyoshi Tamura (b. 1933), based in France, and Mamoru Suganuma (b. 1942).

Ki Society Aikidō. This school of Aikidō was established by Kō-ichi Tōhei (b. 1920) following his acrimonious split from the Aikikai in 1974. As the name implies, Tōhei emphasizes ai-*ki*-dō, placing *ki* at the heart of every technique. Tōhei devised a number of exercises to "test" one's understanding of *ki* principles (these exercises are taught to anyone who is interested, not just Aikidō people), and the technical style is generally rather soft and relaxed.

Yoshinkan Aikidō. This school is based on the hard-hitting Ai-kidō of Gōzō Shioda (1915–1994). Yoshinkan Aikidō tends to be more static in movement and more aggressive with *atemi* than other forms, and the training is more militaristic—Yoshinkan Aikidō is the style taught to Japanese Police Agency recruits. *Hakama* are not worn much in Yoshinkan dōjō.

While Aikidō is always evolving, many aspects of the art have a timeless, universal quality. Many of the techniques are still practiced much the same way as Morihei executed them more than a half-century ago.

Tomiki Aikidō and Yoseikan Budō. Kenji Tomiki (1900–1979), one of Morihei's first students, was also a high-ranking Jūdō instructor, and he attempted to combine Aikidō and Jūdō (against the express wishes of Morihei). The Aikidō techniques of Tomiki Aikidō are similar to those taught by Shirata and Shioda (who trained under Morihei in the same prewar period), but the inclusion of contests based on Jūdō-style competitions into "Aikidō" was widely criticized. Recently, however, some Tomiki Aikidō schools have largely eliminated contests and follow much the same noncompetitive approach as other schools. Another old-time Jūdō man, Minoru Mochizuki (b. 1907), who trained under Morihei for some years, founded Yoseikan Budō, a rigorous system of self-defense.

In addition, there are a large number of other independent and/or unaffiliated Aikidō schools operating in the United States; nearly all of them, however, trace their lineage back to one of the styles mentioned above. It is not uncommon nowadays to run across schools teaching Aiki-Jutsu, usually basing their instruction on one of the many Daitō-Ryū lineages. Sokaku Takeda reportedly had thirty thousand students, and quite of few of his senior disciples created Daitō-Ryū offshoots, some of which now have branch dōjō in the United States. Note, however, that Aiki-Jutsu, Daitō-Ryū style or otherwise, is not—and never has been—synonymous with the art of Aikidō, as conceived of and handed down by Morihei Ueshiba.

Because Aikidō originated in Japan, the initial generation of instructors were naturally all Japanese. Now that Aikidō is becoming established as an integral part of world culture—there are, for example, more Aikidō dōjō in France than there are in Japan—an instructor's nationality has nothing to do with his or her qualification to teach. (This is true even in Japan; the author is one of several foreigners who have served as chief instructors at Japanese dōjō.) Thus, it is no longer appropriate to describe Aikidō as a "Japanese" martial art. "Aikidō" should just be Aikidō, a universal concept like "Yoga" or "Zen" that transcends national borders, and is recognized and appreciated everywhere.

Resources

This is a selected list of the most useful and informative resources for the study of Aikidō. (All the material mentioned here as well as a number of technical videos on Aikidō, may be ordered from *Aikidō Today Magazine* Book and Video Service, P.O. Box 1060, Claremont, CA 91711-1060, U.S.A. The customer order telephone number is (800) 445-2454; the FAX number is (909) 398-1840.)

MORIHEI UESHIBA

Abundant Peace: Morihei Ueshiba, Founder of Aikidō, by John Stevens (Boston: Shambhala Publications, 1987). The first full-length biography of Morihei Ueshiba in English. A revised and expanded edition entitled *Invincible Warrior: An Illustrated Biography of Morihei Ueshiba* is forthcoming from Shambhala Publications.

Three Budō Masters: Kanō (Jūdō), Funakoshi (Karate), Ueshiba (Aikidō), by John Stevens (Tōkyō: Kōdansha International, 1995). Compares the lives and teachings of these three great modern masters.

Aikidō Masters: Prewar Students of Morihei Ueshiba (Tōkyō: Aiki News, 1993). Contains interesting information on Morihei and the early days of Aikidō.

Aiki News Morihei Ueshiba Video Biography: vol. 1, *Aiki Budō* (early career); vol. 2, *Takemusu Aiki* (the years 1952–1958); vol. 3, *Rendez-vous with Adventure* (1958 U.S. television documentary); vol. 4, *Way of Harmony* (1958–1962); vol. 5, *Divine Techniques* (final years, 1962–1969); vol. 6, *The Founder of Aikidō* (1961 Japanese television documentary, with English translation).

THE ART OF AIKIDŌ

Budō: Teachings of the Founder of Aikidō, introduction by Kisshōmaru Ueshiba, translation by John Stevens (Tōkyō: Kōdansha International, 1991). A translation of the teaching manual *Budō*, with photographs of Morihei demonstrating the techniques, plus many other technical photographs from the Noma Dōjō series, presents the reader with the opportunity to train under the Founder himself.

Aikidō: The Way of Harmony, by John Stevens, under the direction of Rinjirō Shirata (Boston: Shambhala Publications, 1984). Outlines the techniques of Classical Aikidō.

Aikidō, by Kisshōmaru Ueshiba (Tōkyō: Hōzansha, 1985). The basic primer of Aikikai Hombu Dōjō style Aikidō.

Traditional Aikidō: Sword, Stick, and Body Arts, 5 vols. (Tōkyō: Sugawara Martial Arts Institute, 1973–1976), and *Takemusu Aikidō*, 2 vols. (Tōkyō: Aiki News, 1994–1995), by Morihiro Saitō. Iwama-style Aikidō.

Dynamic Aikidō, by Gōzō Shioda (Tōkyō: Kōdansha International, 1968). Outlines the Yoshinkan view of Aikidō.

This Is Aikidō, by Kōichi Tōhei (Tōkyō: Japan Publications, 1975). A manual of *ki*-style Aikidō. Unfortunately, it is out of print, but copies can usually be located at larger libraries. Recent editions of other books by Tōhei that are available are *Ki in Daily Life* (Tōkyō: Japan Publications, 1994) and *The Book of Ki* (Tōkyō: Japan Publications, 1994).

Aikidō: Tradition and New Tomiki Free Fighting Method, by Nobuyoshi Higashi (New York: Unique Publications, 1989). Heavy duty Tomiki style *budō*.

The Principles of Aikidō, by Mitsugi Saotome (Boston: Shambhala Publications, 1993). A teaching manual by the chief instructor of the Aikidō Schools of Ueshiba.

Ultimate Aikidō, by Yoshimitsu Yamada (New York: Citadel Press, 1994). A manual by one of the senior instructors of the United States Aikidō Federation.

Aikidō and the Dynamic Sphere, by A. Westbrook and O. Ratti (Rutland, Vt.: Tuttle, 1970). One of the first instruction manuals to appear, the text is now a bit outdated, but the book's graphic illustrations have become classics.

Aikidō: The Heavenly Road, by Kenji Shimizu (Chicago: Editions q, Inc., 1994). Shimizu, one of the last direct students of Morihei Ueshiba, established his own organization called Tendō-Ryū Aikidō in 1982.

THE PHILOSOPHY OF AIKIDŌ

The Essence of Aikidō: Spiritual Teachings of Morihei Ueshiba, compiled by John Stevens (Tōkyō: Kōdansha International, 1993), and *The Secrets of Aikidō* by John Stevens (Boston: Shambhala Publications, 1995), are indispensible for the study of Aikidō philosophy. Both books also contain extensive sections on Aikidō techniques. An audiotape on *kototama* chanting titled *Kototama: The Secret Sounds of Aikidō,* recorded by John Stevens, is available from the *Aikidō Today Magazine* Book & Video Service. Beginning students, however, may want to start with *The Art of Peace,* by Morihei Ueshiba, translated by John Stevens (Boston: Shambhala Publications, 1992), and *The Spirit of Aikidō,* by Kisshōmaru Ueshiba (Tōkyō: Kōdansha International, 1984), which are more accessible. Also good for Aikidō philosophy are *Aikidō and the Harmony of Nature,* by Mitsugi Saotome (Boston: Shambhala Publications, 1993), and *It's a Lot Like Dancing,* by Terry Dobson, Rikki Moss, and Jan Watson (Berkeley, Calif.: Frog, Ltd., 1994).

SCHOOLS AND STYLES AND GENERAL INFORMATION

Aikidō Today Magazine (P.O. Box 1060, Claremont, CA 91711-1060), the only international non-partisan journal devoted exclusively to Aikidō, publishes a wide variety of articles on Aikidō and interviews with top Aikidō instructors from all over the world. Each issue additionally includes an extensive "Calendar of Events." ATM also annually publishes an updated Dōjō Directory. Two good books for beginning students are *The Aikidō Student Handbook* (Berkeley, Calif.: Frog, Ltd., 1993) and *Aikidō for Life* by Gaku Homma (Berkeley, Calif.: North Atlantic Books, 1990). Other books of general interest are *Aikidō and the New Warrior*, edited by Richard S. Heckler (Berkeley, Calif.: North Atlantic Books, 1985); *Women in Aikidō*, by Andrea Siegal (Berkeley, Calif.: North Atlantic Books, 1993); *Aikidō in America*, by John Stone and Ron Meyer, (Berkeley, Calif.: Frog Ltd., 1995); and *Children and the Martial Arts*, by Gaku Homma (Berkeley, Calif.: North Atlantic Books, 1993).

Glossary

In addition to terms mentioned in the text, this glossary also includes other words commonly encountered in Aikidō.

AI Harmony, coming together, unification, integration.

AI (different character with same pronunciation) Love.

AI HANMI Mutual stance with partners facing each other with the same foot forward.

AIKI The blending of two (or more) energies, harmonization, perfect integration.

AIKI-BUDŌ Name used to describe Morihei Ueshiba's art in the prewar period.

AIKIDŌ "The Way of Harmony," the art founded by Morihei Ueshiba.

AIKIDŌKA Aikidō practitioner.

AIKI JINJA The aiki shrine Morihei Ueshiba had built in Iwama, Ibaragi Prefecture, Japan.

AIKI-JŌ Staff techniques according to Aikidō principles.

AIKI-JUTSU/AIKI-JŪJUTSU Martial art systems based on *aiki* timing and control.

AIKIKAI The largest Aikidō organization, headed by Kisshōmaru Ueshiba, Morihei Ueshiba's son and successor as *dōshu*.

AIKI-KEN Swordsmanship according to Aikidō principles.

AIKI Ō-KAMI Great Spirit of Aiki, the all-inclusive spirit of Aikidō, the supreme symbol of Aikidō ideals.

119

AIKI TAISO Aikidō warm-up exercises.

AI-NUKI Simultaneous escape, mutual preservation, the goal of Aikidō.

AI-UCHI Simultaneous striking, mutual destruction, the negation of Aikidō.

AME-NO-MURAKUMO-KUKI-SAMUHARA-RYŪ-Ō This is name of Morihei's guardian angel, the "Heavenly, Awesome, and Enlightened Dragon King"; Morihei himself as an idealized spirit.

AME-NO-UKIHASHI "Floating bridge of heaven"; symbolizes the link between the material and the spiritual realms of existence.

ARIGATŌ GOZAIMASHITA "Thank you very much," Japanese expression exchanged between instructors and students at the conclusion of training.

ASHI Leg or foot.

ATEMI Strike, a blow directed toward an anatomical weak point; used defensively in Aikidō.

AWASE Blending; drawing out one's partner by initiating the technique.

BOKKEN Wooden sword.

BUDŌ Modern Japanese martial disciplines.

BUDŌKA Martial art practitioner.

BUJUTSU Classical Japanese martial arts.

BUSHIDŌ Classical warrior code of Japan.

BUSHIN "Martial spirit," the highest level of mastery in martial arts.

CHINKON KISHIN "Calming the spirit and returning to the source," an Aikidō meditation technique.

CHI-NO-KOKYŪ "The breath of earth," the second level of Aikidō breathing techniques.

CHOKUSEN-NO-IRMI Direct entering completely behind an attack.

CHŪDAN Middle-level position (of hands, sword, etc.).

DAITŌ-RYŪ A martial art system taught by Sōkaku Takeda.

DAN Rank; in Aikidō the ranking system runs from *shodan* (first degree) through *jūdan* (tenth degree).

DEGUCHI, ONISABURŌ (1871–1947) Ōmoto-kyō leader and Shintō shaman who was Morihei Ueshiba's main guru.

DESHI Disciple.

DŌ A particular path of physical and spiritual refinement; a way of life.

DŌ-GI Training uniform used by martial arts practitioners.

DŌJŌ Training hall.

DŌKA "Songs of the Way," the didactic poems of Morihei Ueshiba.

DORI (also pronounced *tori*) Hold, grab.

DŌSA Basic movements; more commonly *kihon-dōsa*.

DŌSHU Grandmaster; highest position in the Aikikai. Morihei Ueshiba was the first *dōshu*, and his son, Kisshōmaru, is the second, current *dōshu*.

EN-NO-IRIMI Circular entry; entering behind an attack and controlling it in a circular motion.

FUDŌ-NO-SHISEI "Immovable" (firm and steady) posture.

FUDŌ-SHIN "Steadfast spirit"; unassailable presence of mind.

FUKUSHIDOIN First-level instructor.

FURI-TAMA "Shaking down the spirit," a common Aikidō meditation technique adopted from ancient Shintō ritual.

GAKU Horizontal signboard, displaying the name of the *dōjō* or a philosophical aphorism.

GASSHUKU Intensive training session lasting several days. *Gasshuku* is usually translated into English as "camp."

GEDAN Lower-level position.

GI Training uniform.

GODAN Fifth-degree black belt.

GOKYŌ Pinning technique number five.

GYAKU-HANMI Reverse stance in which partners have the opposite foot forward.

HACHIDAN Eighth-degree black belt.

HAKAMA Samurai "skirt" worn by Aikidō and Kendō practitioners.

HANMI Half-open, triangular stance.

HANMI-HANDACHI Techniques in which the *nage* sits while the *uke* stands.

HANTAI Reverse, opposite.

HARA Belly, center of the body.

HENKA-WAZA Techniques exploring possible variations.

HIDARI Left.

HOMBU DŌJŌ Headquarters dōjō of the Aikikai, located in Tōkyō.

IAI-DŌ The art of drawing and cutting with the sword.

IKI Breath; the physical act of respiration.

IKKYŌ Pinning technique number one.

IRIMI "Entering," physically and spiritually, into an opposing force in order to defuse and neutralize it.

IRIMI-NAGE "Entering throw," one of the pillars of technical Aikidō.

IRIMI-TENKAN "Enter and turn," pivoting around a stable center to create Aikidō techniques.

IWAMA Town in Ibaragi Prefecture; location of the Morihei Ueshiba's Aiki Shrine, outdoor dōjō, and farm.

JIN-NO-KOKYŪ The breath of a human being; the third stage in breath meditation.

JIYŪ-WAZA Free-style techniques.

JŌ Four-foot wooden staff.

JŌDAN Upper-level position.

JŌ-DORI Techniques for disarming an opponent armed with a *jō*.

JŌ-TAI-KEN Training with the *jō* paired against the sword.

JŪ The principle of flexibility; the willow aspect of Aikidō techniques and philosophy.

JŪDAN Tenth-degree black belt (the highest rank awarded).

JŪDŌ Modern martial art system established by Jigorō Kanō (1860–1938).

JŪJI-NAGE Crossed-arm throw.

JŪJUTSU Japanese unarmed fighting systems.

KAISO Founder; used in reference to Morihei Ueshiba, founder of Aikidō.

KAITEN "Open and turn," the third pillar of technical Aikidō.

KAKEJIKU Hanging scroll.

KAMAE Stance; "combative" posture.

KAMI God, deity, divine spirit, holy inspiration, guardian angel, enlightened human being.

KAMIZA The front of the *dōjō* where scrolls, photographs of the Founder, and so on, are displayed.

KANSHA Deep and heartfelt gratitude.

KARATE Modern martial art system originating in Okinawa, introduced to the world by Gichin Funakoshi (1868–1957).

KATA "Fixed form," predetermined practice patterns used as a learning vehicle.

KATA-DORI Shoulder grab.

KATATE-DORI Held by one hand.

KATSUHAYABI "Victory right here, right now"; a principal tenet of Aikidō paired with *masakatsu agatsu*.

KEIKO Training; the meaning of *keiko* is, "Use accumulated wisdom to illuminate the present."

KEN Sword.

KENDŌ Modern Japanese swordplay, largely practiced as a competitive sport.

KI (*Ch'i* in Chinese) Vital energy, life force; also the *ki* aspect of Aikidō techniques and philosophy.

KIAI Piercing shout; full-spirited approach to the technique being applied.

KIKAI TANDEN A human being's physical and spiritual center, located about two inches beneath the navel.

KI-NO-NAGARE Free-flowing techniques.

KIMUSUBI The linking of *ki*, the blending of energies.

KŌBUKAN DŌJŌ The name of Morihei's original training hall in Tōkyō.

KOGI-FUNE-UNDŌ "Rowing the boat," an Aikidō warm-up exercise adopted from Shinto-*misogi* ritual.

KŌHAI Junior; one with less Aikidō experience; opposed to *sempai*.

KOJIKI "Records of Ancient Matters," compiled in 712, relates the spiritual history of Japan. It was one of Morihei's favorite books and his lectures often referred to deities and events mentioned in the *Kojiki*.

KOKYŪ Animating breath, life breath of the cosmos; technically, "good timing."

KOKYŪ-HŌ Special exercises to foster breath power.

KOKYŪ-ROKU Breath power as distinguished from raw physical power.

KOKYŪ-UNDŌ Breath movement exercises, performed sitting and standing.

KON The diamond aspect of Aikidō techniques and philosophy.

KOSHI-NAGE Hip throw.

KOTE-GAESHI Wrist turn, a basic Aikidō throwing technique.

KOTOTAMA (also *kotodama*) "Word-spirits," the esoteric science of sacred sound and speech.

KŪ Emptiness; the void that is created by Aikidō countermoves.

KUDEN "Secret teachings," imparted by word of mouth; implies direct, person-to-person, heart-to-heart transmission.

KŪKAI (774–835) The first patriarch of Japanese Shingon Buddhism, founder of the great monastery on Mount Kōya.

KUMANO Ancient district in Wakayama Prefecture, considered the home of Japanese spirituality.

KUMI-JŌ Paired partner training with the *jō*.

KUMI-TACHI Paired partner training with swords.

KYŪ Preliminary grades below *dan* ranking.

KYŪDAN Ninth-degree black belt.

MA-AI Proper interval between two partners; perfect spacing.

MAKOTO-NO-KOKYŪ "True breath," the third stage of breath meditation (same as *jin-no-kokyū*).

MANDALA Sacred diagram; cosmic map.

MASAKATSU AGATSU "True victory is self-victory," one of the principal tenets of Aikidō.

MEN-UCHI Strike to the head or face.

MIGI Right.

MINAKATA, KUMAGUSU (1867–1941) Eccentric scholar and environmentalist who influenced the young Morihei Ueshiba.

MISOGI Purification of body and mind.

MOKUSŌ "Meditate!" a command given to initiate group meditation.

MOROTE-DORI Held by two hands on one arm.

MOUNT KŌYA Headquarters of Shingon Buddhism in Japan.

MUNADORI Chest grab.

NAGARE Flow; unbroken flow of *ki* during the execution of a technique.

NAGE "The one who throws," the defender who applies the technique against the attacker.

NANADAN Seventh-degree black belt; also *shichi-dan.*

NIDAN Second-degree black belt.

NIKKYŌ Pinning technique number two.

NOMA DŌJŌ Training hall owned by Seiji Noma, an early supporter of Morihei Ueshiba and one of Japan's most important publishers; many technical photographs were taken here c. 1936.

OBI Training uniform belt; *kuro-obi* is "black belt."

OMOTE The forward-moving aspect of a technique; the converse of *ura.*

ŌMTO-KYŌ The shamanistic new religion established by Nao Deguchi and Onisaburō Deguchi in the early twentieth century, headquartered in Ayabe, near Kyōto.

ONEGAI-SHIMASU "I ask you please," Japanese expression used between instructor and students at the beginning of training. It expresses the sentiment: "Let's help one another train."

ONE POINT To remain centered; a central concept of Ki Aikidō.

OSAE-WAZA Pinning techniques, one of the pillars of technical Aikidō.

Ō-SENSEI "Great Teacher," the customary way of referring to Morihei Ueshiba among Aikidō practitioners.

ŌYŌ-WAZA Techniques with practical application as self-defense.

RANDORI Free-style techniques against multiple attackers.

REI Bow, the formal gesture of respect used by Aikidō and other *budō* practitioners; also, the command given at the commencement of training.

REIGI Etiquette.

ROKUDAN Sixth-degree black belt.

RYŌTE-DORI Held by both hands.

RYŪ The flowing aspect of Aikidō techniques and philosophy.

RYŪ (different character/same pronunciation) School, tradition (as in Daitō-Ryū).

SAHŌ Etiquette used in performing bows, handling the *jō* and *ken,* and so forth.

SANDAN Third-degree black belt.

SANKAKU-IRIMI Triangular entering (also known as *issoku-irimi,* "one-step *irimi"*).

SANKYŌ Pinning technique number three.

SEIZA "Correct and quiet sitting," samurai style of sitting with the legs tucked beneath the buttocks.

SEMPAI Senior in Aikidō experience; opposed to *kohai*.

SENSEI Teacher; term of respect added to the name of an instructor.

SHIAI Contest, organized competition.

SHIAI (different characters with the same pronunciation) "Encounter with death," a concept symbolizing the necessity of full concentration and absolute attention when practicing Aikidō.

SHIDOIN Senior instructor.

SHIHAN Master teacher; used for instructors of the highest ranks.

SHIHŌ-GIRI "Four-directions cut," the initiating move of *aiki-ken*.

SHIHŌ-NAGE "Four-directions throw," one of the pillars of technical Aikidō.

SHIKKŌ Knee-walking; an exercise used to build leg and hip strength.

SHINBU FUSATSU "Divine techniques do not kill," a key tenet in Aikidō philosophy.

SHINGON The Tantric Buddhism of Japan.

SHINKEN SHŌBU "Fight to the finish," used figuratively in Aikidō to mean "to throw oneself single-mindedly into one's training."

SHINTŌ "Way of the Gods," the traditional religion of Japan; a combination of nature worship, animism, Taoism, and shamanism.

SHODAN First degree; initial black-belt ranking.

SHŌMEN The front of the *dōjō* where the *kamiza* is located.

SHŌMEN-UCHI A direct strike to the head.

SHUGYŌ Intensive training; lifelong discipline.

SOTO Outside.

SUBURI Sword or *jō* movements practiced individually; also repetitive cuts of the sword or *jō*.

SUMŌ Traditional Japanese wrestling; associated with Shintō mythology.

SUWARI-WAZA Seated techniques.

TACHI-DORI Techniques used to counter a sword attack.

TAI-JUTSU Unarmed body-techniques.

TAI-NO-HENKŌ "Pivoting of the body," a basic Aikidō movement.

TAI-SABAKI Body movements.

TAKEDA, SOKAKU (1859–1943) Grandmaster of the Daitō-Ryū and principal *budō* tacher of Morihei Ueshiba.

TAKEMUSU AIKI "Courageous and creative living," the motto of Aikidō.

TANABE Seaside town in Wakayama Prefecture; birthplace of Morihei Ueshiba.

TANDEN Center of the body just below the navel; the place of "one point."

TANINSU-GAKE Free-style techniques against multiple attackers.

TANREN "Forging the body and mind," especially intensive training.

TANTŌ-DORI Techniques used to counter a knife attack.

TANTRA Esoteric science; a complex system of techniques designed to liberate the mind and body.

TATAMI Mats used to cover the *dōjō* floor.

TEGATANA Hand sword.

TEKUBI Wrist, as in *ushiro tekubi-dori,* "wrists held from behind."

TENCHI Heaven and earth.

TENCHI-NAGE "Heaven-and-earth throw," a fundamental Aikidō technique.

TEN-NO-KOKYŪ "Breath of heaven," the first stage of breath meditation.

TOBU-UKEMI "Flying break-fall," in which one turns over in the air before (softly) landing on the mat.

TORI "The one who takes" the technique; alternate term for *nage,* the defender.

TSUKI Thrust; punch to the head or stomach.

UCHI Inside.

UCHI (different character with same pronunciation) Strike or blow to the head or body.

UCHI-DESHI Live-in disciple who trains full-time under a senior instructor's direction.

UCHI-GATAME "Pounding the body with the fists," a warm-up exercise used to stimulate the skin and muscles.

UKE "The one who receives" the technique; the attacker.

UKEMI Break-fall; *mae-ukemi,* break-fall to the front; *ushiro-ukemi,* break-fall to the rear.

URA Back, reverse; the converse of *omote.*

USHIRO-DORI Held from behind.

USHIRO-WAZA "Rear techniques," one of the pillars of technical Aikidō.

WAZA Techniques.

YOBI-DASHI "Calling out," a preemptive strike intended to neutralize an attack before it starts to develop.

YODAN Fourth-degree black belt; also *yondan.*

YOGA A system of physical and spiritual development originating in India.

YOKOMEN-UCHI Diagonal strike to the side of the head or neck.

YONKYŌ Pinning technique number four.

YŪDANSHA One with *dan* ranking; black belt.

ZANSHIN Unbroken concentration; remaining alert and on guard even after the throw or pin is completed.

ZEN A Buddhist meditation system emphasizing direct realization.

Credits

Index